Ship To:

AP-TP - 1033647-1-1315
Main Address
800 Avondale Ave
1033647-1-1315
Grandview Heights, OH 43212

Buyer PO #: 1033647-1-1315

Order ID: 113-6834435-2339459

Thank you for buying from Vashon Island Books on Amazon Marketplace.

Shipping Address:	Order Date:	Wed, Jul 8, 2026
AP-TP	Shipping Service:	Standard
Main Address	Buyer Name:	CollegeBooksDirect
800 Avondale Ave	Seller Name:	Vashon Island Books
1033647-1-1315		
Grandview Heights, OH		
43212		

Quantity	Product Details
1	Radiant Measures [Paperback] [1999] James, Gurley **SKU:** 0707921 **ASIN:** 0964719967 **Condition:** Used - Very Good **Order Item ID:** 164312755417961

RADIANT MEASURES

RADIANT MEASURES

James Gurley

Acknowledgments

The author is grateful to the journals where these poems, sometimes in other versions, first appeared:

Arc: "Biophilia"
LitRag: "Illuminated Mechanisms"
Event: "Variations on a Theme by Kandinsky"
Luna: "The Life of Objects"
Milestone Review: "Chemical Romance of the Leaf"
Poetry: "Biosophy, an Optimist's Manifesto"
Poetry Newsletter: "The Nature of Colors"
Poetry Northwest: "On the Theory of Transformation"
Prism International: "A Temporal Bestiary"
Switched-On Gutenberg: "73 Octaves of Nature"
Terrain: "The World, or Instability"

Pontoon, Number One: an anthology of Washington State poets:
"A Temporal Bestiary," "Biophilia," and "The Radius of Metaphor"

ISBN 0-9647199-6-7

The printing of this chapbook was supported, in part, by a special publication grant awarded by the King County Arts Commission.

Cover image: detail from *The Cosmographical Glasse*,
William Cunningham, 1559

Editors: T. Clear, Jeff Crandall, Linda Greenmun,
Peter Pereira, and Gary Winans

Floating Bridge Press • PO Box 18814
Seattle, Washington 98118
www.scn.org/arts/floatingbridge

for Neile

Table of Contents

The Theory of Transformation

Feel how the vertebrae join the ribs
to form a hollow for breathing,
and how when I place my palm
across your breastbone the membrane
of skin barely conceals what lies
underneath, the sinew and marrow
our bodies are made of —
Consider the webs of bone
in our hands and feet
that mimic the folded wings
of some extinct flightless bird,
the braided muscles now fossilized
channels in rock and shadow
laid down by the head and feathers —
How different are these tubular structures,
how alike, these ancestors
whose origin is proof
the syntax bred into us at birth
is not indistinct or random —
When you trace the bend in my elbow,
the soft cartilage at my knees,
the skein of hair tumbling onto my forehead,
you retrace our evolution,
this architecture of spirit and bone,
the spine, the root of our flesh
where you fit your breath into my breath,
my body into your body —
What we believe, stupefied, in that
blind instant, borne up

by the curve of your lips on my tongue,
the twisting of your leg over mine,
is how this pattern of nerves and veins,
fragile net underneath the skin,
descends from some archaic design —
Suddenly we resurface, baffled
how we are shaped for this passage
by the attitude of the pelvis,
amazed that the bow of my arm fits neatly
against your side, amazed
at this radiant measure lying here,
smoothing each other's skin.

Biophilia

— at the conservation reserve outside London, Ontario

The fox came upon us unexpectedly.
He froze and our world
narrowed to a span meters wide.

I heard your words break
into fragments. I felt so uneasy —
something extraordinary in the forest

stood close to where we stood.
His diaphragm rising and falling,
eyes searching for any

movement that might betray us.
The smell of water, the directional
bend of a plant stalk

mattered. I turned my head
and he vanished. Melted
into abstract description,

that's just a metaphor
for slyness, malevolence,
the implicit threat.

All these qualities
he channels into his ability
to stay alert. Alive.

It's nearly dusk, now;
trees suffused with continuous
but dimming light.

We stop by a pond
fringed with larch —
rest; still craving a sense

of the mysterious. Your words
pour in and around me,
and I want to know the touch

of everything. Described this way,
it's nothing but a glimpse
of one small animal. Say it's

only myth: say he looks at us
from his own world. In the end
it's enough to just believe.

— *after E.O. Wilson*

Variation on a Theme by Kandinsky

The thunderous clouds are a collision of worlds.
What Kandinsky saw in painting
as each nostril of the model awakens the same awe
he found in the wild duck's flight, the joining
of leaf and branch, the frog swimming,
the pouch of the pelican.
Slow revelations of our world.
I write these words while outside
wind, light, the furious branches twist
in the storm coming ashore,
and what's set free from the heavy-muscled clouds
are opposites no longer held in balance —
above and below, right and left,
movement and stillness — until the storm abates
in languid and slow clouds, the absence
of movement. I think of Kandinsky improvising
a new composition. Having thrown himself
against the wind's ease he writes: this plane
to the right — centered inwardly is a movement
toward home, to the left — going outward —
is a movement into the distance.
He raises his brush
over the canvas, over the startling
white world he knew as adventurous,
and somehow an invisible and somber power
moves against the chaos.
This storm and its variations, cedars
holding firm against gusts threatening to uproot
everything, how little of it I absorb:

the pigeons that perch under our house's eaves,
pools of water passing cars raise up again,
prisms of rain catching light like drops of color.
My purpose is to find that dark music
the storm brings with it, not as lightning,
but in the branches and trees yielding a path
for disorder in this world
with clues everywhere.
Kandinsky painted lines that veered
into the shape of a horse
(the horse bearing the rider with strength and speed)
and into the free linear structure of a picture:
Little Dream In Red.
I make of this crazy weather
a composition of light and dark, moving across
the white field, wind spiraling
its web of lightning and sound, curious
arc of clouds blossoming with rain.
The point is always to be moving — constantly
in motion — from point and line to plane.
From this, the experience of color coming out
of the tube, sensuous tearing
apart as the storm cuts inland and unleashes
itself, is a curious world. Meanwhile the brush,
as Kandinsky knew, becomes the branch
outside my window, the cacophony a musical sound,
a hissing of colors, alchemy.

The Nature of Colors

— Isaac Newton, 1672

The sun draws a beam
of light through this room
to the bowl of fruit on the table —
apple, plum, apricot, each
take on a new color.
Thus the visible spectrum
reveals itself

in a perpetual tremor. Every object
shimmers with a halo of atoms
pulsing out into space.
When I pass a prism through the beam
invisible threads untangle
like strands of yarn

shaking out the last flames
of the sun. You must love colors
to see what's beautiful
in this world, to name them
as they appear

on the screen,
from violet to red: the reflection
opens new mysteries
that the eye brings together,
the spectrum a coherent
language.

Through a series of prisms
and lens, we learn
these fundamental truths:
light falls
from the heavens, conveys
to us a broken image

and we reconstruct
the world, these topsy-turvy
images from our own
blindness,
from what shines forth.

Illuminating Mechanisms

The tubes glow, warming up; voices
float from my father's dust-covered old Philco.
A grainy mixture of jazz and loud rap
radiates inside the maze of wires and glass.
When I tune in stations the machine keeps tempo
with the even steady ticking of the dial.

I take it apart. Lift off the mahogany frame,
find bits of shiny brass, grease and dust.
Soon, the radio ceases to be itself.
The oscillator, condenser, amplifier,
all those shapes a nostalgia
for discarded things.

Sound crackles, flares
transformed in this tangled garden, waves
humming through tubes to the speaker,
frequencies falling into place out of empty air.
Songs emerge in this circle of yellow
mapping the brightness, a universe
of noise and melody coming in.

The Radius of Metaphor

A stereo blares country western
two houses away, the world's weariness
distilled to a twangy guitar
that embroiders the baseline.
Briefly transformed by the tempo,
I listen to the spaces music
opens and can't close.
The singer who holds onto one note,
his doorway to a place
from which he's been banished.

I tell myself it's intentional.
The garden, the earthworm I dig up,
converts into words. My knees bent
into damp soil, the circle I clear,
filling a bucket with chickweed.
Colorful blossoms slip through
my fingers as I pull weeds.
Outline of buds and branches,
surge of sunlight
against my back when I —

here I stop. Watch my neighbor
hum as he works under the hood of his car,
his socket wrench clicking.

Because it's possible he might
drop his wrench and break my concentration,
because I'm half-dreaming

the girl who wheels her bicycle
past me, yelling for sheer joy I suppose,
because I'm thirsty, I get up,
stand where weeds have tipped over
the bucket. Tendrils cover my sneakers.

Inside our house, the woman
I have loved these long years —
how easy these words are.
Walking into the cool half-light.
Her voice as she pours water
into the blue glass I hold.
Leaning against the fridge, we talk.
Of my sister's illness, a friend's divorce.

Or maybe it's my hand's slow movement
on her back, lifting up her blouse
and rubbing her spine, easing
whatever tension remains between us.
Shh . . . Listen. I close her eyes,
then mine. Are these words enough?
What happens next? The light fades
into dusk on our furniture, sudden quiet.

A Temporal Bestiary

"Beautiful is the still of the night."
— *Georg Trakl, 1887-1914*

We're held by the rhythms of light,
like the fruit bats who fly out to feed

at dusk, rising from the trees
in a gray-brown fury of wings.

We carry these time signals
through our bloodstream, the body's own

clock predicting that behind our house
tonight fireflies will swarm,

their lunar mating rituals triggered
by the synchrony inside each flash,

each insect seeking the harmony
of others, instinct telling them

just this moment of light, this is all.

*

I sit beside you on the damp grass.
It is late, we should be asleep

but a whippoorwill starts up, a dark
portal as his call grows near.

*

What we look upon we take into ourselves,
the pollen-drenched blossoms

shut for business; our cat prowls
the flower beds, her curious chattering

at her prey. My trance broken
by the whirl of moths

around the patio lights,
your voice as you tell me

office gossip, jokes, that our car
needs a tune-up, how your plans

for the weekend include sleeping in.

*

What of those creatures like us
who take their bearing from the sun,

emerging at dawn from the pupa stage,
cousins of the darkness and light,

birds who migrate to subtle
changes in the seasons?

We are bordered by the earth's
steady pull, cool breezes

so you long for a sweater,
and wonder why we are out here.

The fireflies? The summer night sky?

*

We walk back to the lit house.
Muffled suburban noises engulf us

until our voices are mere echoes
of what we've seen, satellite headlines

of war. Disaster. Our lives
flare up in these earthbound days,

the early hours when I can't sleep,
can't stop the great curve of light,

its strange powers, its radiance
edging through our bedroom window.

Weighing the Planets

— at the Instruments of Science Exhibit, National History Museum of Scotland

With one touch I set the heavens
  in motion, on a wire of time
curved within a glass.
  The solar symmetries of our lives

themselves in the turning
  orrery, the orbit gears safely
threading the planets in a whirl
  through an artificial sphere.

Who held these instruments, whose palm
  warmed a polished copper cylinder,
who drew his measure
  with this theodolite in India,

parceling out the wilderness for God
  and Queen? These useless
devices from a ghost-world —
  all that's left of the unconquerable —

now mythical under glass: the sextant,
  the air pump's glass bowl —
there are so many lives' work
  in these tools; how it was to explore

and discover, to subdue the unknown.
  Their stories all but vanished,
the land surveyor hiking up
  a mountain in India

who ignores the ache
  in his left leg as he hums
a hymn for fortitude —
  these adventures and the earth

his, with what amazing ease
  he goes on, mastering
these instruments that are
  immortal even if our lives are not.

The Life of Objects

— Josef Sudek, photographer, Prague, Winter 1946

for Neile

Against the windowsill Sudek places bread,
a vase with flowers, a stone, a piece of paper;

in others we see only condensation,
a thin gauze over the life in his garden.

The light is lyric. The apple tree
a discourse on optics.

Each day his window is a landscape.
Mystery lies in the shadow areas: a paradox

barely visible in clothesline sheets,
spring leaves unfolding the garden,

or in Prague on a chilly day after a late snowfall.
Under the Occupation a camera in the streets

is suspect and old friends vanish.
What does liberation bring? A new regime.

More shortages. And to Sudek this Jew,
Sonja Bullaty, who returns to Prague

from the camps transformed by the illogic
of war into a woman without a family,

who now believes it's good
to feel at home in the darkroom,

a phonograph playing Janacek's beautiful
panoramas. Perhaps they become lovers,

briefly; their union, their passion
reawakens the city, its horizon

a familiar window — rivers, bridges,
clusters of roofs — in the same way the body is

familiar, even if we don't know why pleasure
beckons, the loved one iridescent in the light

and shadows between buildings.
If the war, the new regime, is undone by

what the body helps us forget, it's a life
found in Sudek's photographs, but where?

In these objects? The ecstasy of his garden
he loves, the apple trees, his home,

his obsession? When I see his photographs
I know how the woman I love is linked

forever to the city we've shared.
Mornings we wake early, sun edging over

the mountain rim to our bed, to where
she unwillingly gives up her body to the day,

stretching into it as into a new dress.
And leaves for work before I do,

noisily descending the stairwell
to the street, the shops opening up

amidst the confusion of commerce and cars —
where I lose sight of her.

The ordinariness of this routine somehow
keeps us together. I don't understand

what drew her to me anymore than Sudek did Sonja.
Or how it can burn up a whole city square

not with light, but the sharp taste of her
in my mouth, the sensual late afternoon

outlining downtown in lush colors,
the taverns, banks, offices, streetcars

in a corridor of light, not haze
that swallows us, our house.

Our city so close it seems made
entirely of tenderness and our flesh.

A closeness Sudek must have felt, taking months
or years to print a photograph — believing

only in the spell that overtakes him,
light yielding its secrets so slowly.

73 Octaves of Nature

Lying in the center of the MRI machine,
the ceaseless, metallic banging

courses through your blood.

You must remain still; a technician
charts the magnetic current,

the resonant spectrum now haloed

on a screen. The resonance flares
through your skin, in your veins

so passionately entered.

The harmonics of shifting electrons
reflect the tenacity of bone and muscle.

Your flesh sketched out,

all tones and timbres. The vibrations
map the misshapen pituitary,

the tumor's evidence your doctor calls

benign, some aberrant growth
on your skull's perfect architecture.

These pulses absorb the energy

buried deep inside you, the mystery itself —
how these radio waves, nature's

73 octaves, are almost imperceptible.

We never hear or feel their touch
upon us. A memory or an instinct

to survive. Eyes closed, you see

the image inside your skull,
revealed in the oddly shaded screen.

As fear. As notes that oscillate

between protons and emit signals,
the roar in your ears carried

through the coils and instruments,

where your other self grows
more vivid in a thicket

of frequencies, its music

spreading out over
the landscape of your body.

The World, or Instability

"I wish to sing the changeful ample world . . . "
— *Constantine S. Rafinesque, botanist and archeologist, 1783-1840*

Fatigued after a day's walking, Rafinesque feasts
on corn bread and salt pork.
Wasps assail him like the Furies
while he eats. He presses new plants,
new species in his notebook.
Later a rival botanist determines
they're European weeds.
Hope is like that.
All is new, new, NEW! and sprung out
of the cataclysms of our Earth.
The forces of plenty abound: the world and all within
mutable, the divine instability;
science. I'm guilty as Rafinesque,
preaching on, not telling you
of his umbrella, a constant companion;
the family he abandoned in Italy. How reading this
you might think him cruel to set sail —
A failure. Like this portrait,
leaving out his later years
in a Philadelphia slum, burdened
with his herbarium, his unsold life's work.
I tell you instead of his wanderings —
his mania for naming: Rafinesque head bent
down to an oddly shaped leaf,
a small man in a coat of yellow nankeen
stained all over with sap.

Out Walking

> "Suppose we saw ourselves burning
> like maples in a golden autumn."
> — *Loren Eiseley*

for Robin Skelton

It begins with the bones, our uncertainties
  deep in the marrow. We seek the forest
quiet, stones warmed by afternoon sun —
  these pleasures found in walking
with a sweater wrapped around our hips,
  a breeze casting about the bright,
dying leaves. We name what we find:
  discarded snail shell, wild blackberries
just ripening. A bird up in the trees
  somewhere sings his only world, sings
the ferns and salal undergrowth.
  We come out of habit for the rituals
of spirits haunting our earth.
  Aren't they really a parallel life?
A dream, the unconscious? The faulty tale
  of our faith in our own flesh.
Betrayed by our own vigil, we stand
  as a deer noses grass ahead,
the neighbor cat stalks her prey,
  chirping to hypnotize it.
We're sun-struck with these gifts.
  This sudden blazing overcomes us.
What then? There is beauty in cool evenings
  and harvest celebrations, the fall
colors intensified in crisp air. Our late

happiness has come. Our world,
October at its center, given, the
first chapters in an unfinished life.

Chemical Romance of the Leaf

Chlorophyll — a green so common
it's not a color, but a web holding our world
together. It starts in the rangy weeds
of my garden absorbing light. Lilacs, roses,
the mock orange, new shoots, appetite
ravenous. This chemical pattern
so beautiful, outside on a warm spring day,
planting lobelia and sweet alyssum,
pulling off my jacket in the heat.
I get up, wander to the alley.
Garbage cans and junked cars, an old dog
that barks at a cat who taunts it.
This kitsch we all live with. That a man
nearly forty can build his days around,
a breeze in the leaves, their color,
these beliefs I count on, quietly, gratefully —
how else can I learn my life?

Let me start again.
Take this half-filled sheet, hold it up
before me, and look past its edge at the trees —
vertical lines of black ink blurring
to the dark bars of their trunks.
This loosening of focus, a passageway into
leaves crackling in my hands, the geometric graces
of branches, a living maze stretching beyond
my sight. I stole from the land
these words, this invitation to reverie.
My table overlooks a small garden,

a screen of hawthorns and maples
blocking off ugly cement.
I ask myself just how leaves
change color, the burst of light
received inside. I've a beginner's
faith in things unseen.

Biosophy, an Optimist's Manifesto

> "The purpose of life is life itself — and when we have done our share inwardly, the outer things will follow of themselves."
> — *Goethe, letter to Heinrich Meyer, August 8, 1792*

Say it's naive, this belief
in more than Darwin's old manifesto

combat, the wolf who attacks by instinct,
the struggle of a viper cornering

his prey, our being defined by this way
of knowing the earth. What of that

other possibility, evening,
when our whole body is one sense,

the sky spreading out its liberation
in great splashes of phosphorous,

of the Bible, the prophets,
the oldest poems, the stony shore

of the pond, pebbles underfoot sounding
like a string quartet by Beethoven

in my head, this unabashed
enthusiasm in the capricious loops

and detours we take, eating wild berries,
their succulence a thirst

for the sky, its mackerel clouds,
lit from within, the city

wavering in the distance like the cosmos,
for the owl hidden in the trees,

for barn swallows moving in and out
of our path, in the quiet, love,

where this closeness, this nonsense
takes hold: like joy. These words

a shoreline where we can stand.
Slender ribbons of grass at our shoes

cleanse us, so we imagine.
We're like one of those poems

that doesn't know where it's going,
like the hummingbird in our garden

searching for the showiest hibiscus
to slake its hunger. Tired, we walk

through damp grass, a country we explore.
We're drawn to this circle of intimacy,

for such momentary peace the body
still holds true. We breathe

in its grace, the night-blooming flowers
another way of knowing the world.

NOTES

"The Life of Objects": One of Czechoslovakia's most gifted photographers, Josef Sudek (1896-1976) was an integral part of the literary scene in Prague. After the war, he took on as his assistant Sonja Bullaty, a concentration camp survivor. Bullaty later left Europe for America and became a champion of Sudek's work. Sudek's obsession was to capture the beauty in his beloved city of Prague.

"The World, or Instability": Now largely forgotten, Constantine Rafinesque's botanical work foreshadowed in part the notion of adaptation in nature later crucial to Darwin. Rafinesque also composed a 300-page poem in which he tried to explain the philosophical and scientific basis for his theories on the mutability of species.

"Chemical Romance of the Leaf": This poem draws its title from an essay written early in this century by Dr. H.E. Armstrong, addressing the philosophical comforts found in our awareness of the natural cycles around us and in the chemical basis for all life.

§

James Gurley lives in Seattle, and works as a librarian. He has held grants from Seattle Arts Commission, King County Arts Commission, and Artist Trust. He is an associate editor for the Seattle e-zine *Salmon Bay Review*. He has also previously published a chapbook, *Transformations*, with Reference West in 1995.

This chapbook was formatted in Adobe PageMaker, and offset-printed on acid-free recycled paper in an edition of 400. The typeface is Adobe Garamond.

This is number 113 of 400.